SMALL TREASURES FROM SCRAPS

More SIMPLY CHARMING Quilts

Tara Lynn Darr

SMALL TREASURES FROM SCRAPS

More **SIMPLY CHARMING** *Quilts*

By Tara Lynn Darr

Editor: Kimber Mitchell
Designer: Bob Deck
Photography: Aaron T. Leimkuehler
Illustration: Lon Eric Craven
Technical Editor: Deanna Hodson
Photo Editor: Jo Ann Groves

Published by:
Kansas City Star Books
1729 Grand Blvd.
Kansas City, Missouri, USA 64108

First edition, first printing

ISBN: 9780970913166

Library of Congress Control Number: 2014932653

Printed in the United States of America by Walsworth Publishing Co., Marceline, MO

To order copies, call StarInfo at (816) 234-4473.

ACKNOWLEDGMENTS

To my wonderful family for all the support you have given me along the quilted trail. Even when I'm frazzled and knee-deep in deadlines for my next book or project, you are still troopers. For the many dinners you made for yourselves, the trips to the grocery store, and for just figuring it all out for yourselves while I worked, I thank you. I love you and appreciate everything you do for me.

To my sweet friends in the quilting industry. You are my rock when I'm in a hard place, my bumper to throw ideas off of, and an open ear when I just want to whine. You girls know who you are, and you rock the quilting industry. I'm proud and thankful to call you friends.

To Kimber Mitchell, my editor and fellow quilt lover. Thank you again for making the book writing process an easy one. You keep me on track and perfect my imperfect writing. Your ability to help me express myself through the written word is priceless.

To Aaron Leimkueler, photographer extraordinaire. What a treasure you are. I do believe I should come take photography lessons from you!

To Lon Eric Craven, my illustrator, thank you for doing just what you do perfectly. I wish I had your abilities to work the magic that you do in such a short time.

To Bob Deck, book design guru. Your creative skills and abilities amaze me. Thank you for bringing this book to life with but a few scraps of fabric.

To Doug Weaver for once again believing in me and giving me such a wonderful opportunity. By allowing me to write the books I do, you make my heart happy and my family elated. This book-writing gig allows me to continue working at home as I have done since my children were born. Thank you for keeping that dream alive and my priorities straight.

DEDICATION

Thank you to each of the wonderful quilters in my family. Each of you has touched me, helped me to grow as a quilter, and inspired me to do the things in life I love the most. I hope to pass this quilting legacy on to my own family so it can live on for generations to come. As I continue to study my family history, I learn more and more about the quilters in my family's past who are no longer with us. Someday I hope to gather enough information and photos of these outstanding women and their creativity to share with the world in a future book. I am so grateful to these remarkable women for teaching their daughters, cousins, friends, and other family members to quilt. They didn't know it at the time, but they helped shape the person I am today—not only a quilter but one from a long line of creative women I'm proud of in every way. I wish I could have met them all.

ABOUT THE AUTHOR

Tara Lynn Darr comes from a long line of quilters. Growing up in a tiny town in Indiana, she often visited family members who quilted and sewed. As an adult, she turned her love of sewing into a cottage industry, making dolls and other creations from her home and selling them at craft fairs. Eventually, she moved to Joliet, Illinois, where she currently resides with her husband, two children, and a lovable family basset hound.

Tara's passion for quilting was sparked in 1999, when a friend invited her to attend an international quilt show. Since then, quilting and crafting have opened many doors of opportunity. She now designs her own patterns through her Sew Unique Creations pattern company. Tara's designs have also been published in *American Patchwork & Quilting* magazine, *Simply Charming: Small Scrap Quilts of Yesteryear*, and *Cozy Quilts: A Charming Blend of Wool Appliqué and Cotton Patchwork*. She also wrote a book on rug hooking and has self-published two of her own quilting books.

You can find Tara at many of the national quilting shows, selling fabrics, notions, and patterns that have tickled her fancy. When she's not traveling to quilt shows, blogging, Facebooking, or playing in a pile of fabric, she enjoys creating quilts inspired by the past, hand-piecing quilts, reading, cooking, visiting family members, and riding her four-wheeler down dirt roads and trails.

For more information on Tara's designs, visit her website at www.sewuniquecreations.com, her blog at www.sewuniquecreations.blogspot.com, or her Facebook page where she enjoys the lively banter of her many quilting friends. You can find her on Facebook by entering her business name, Sew Unique Creations, in the search box.

Someday, Tara hopes to enjoy a slow-paced life in the Appalachian Mountains surrounded by its beautiful scenery while operating a destination quilt shop on her property. She also dreams of finishing and publishing the witty quilting novel she is currently writing.

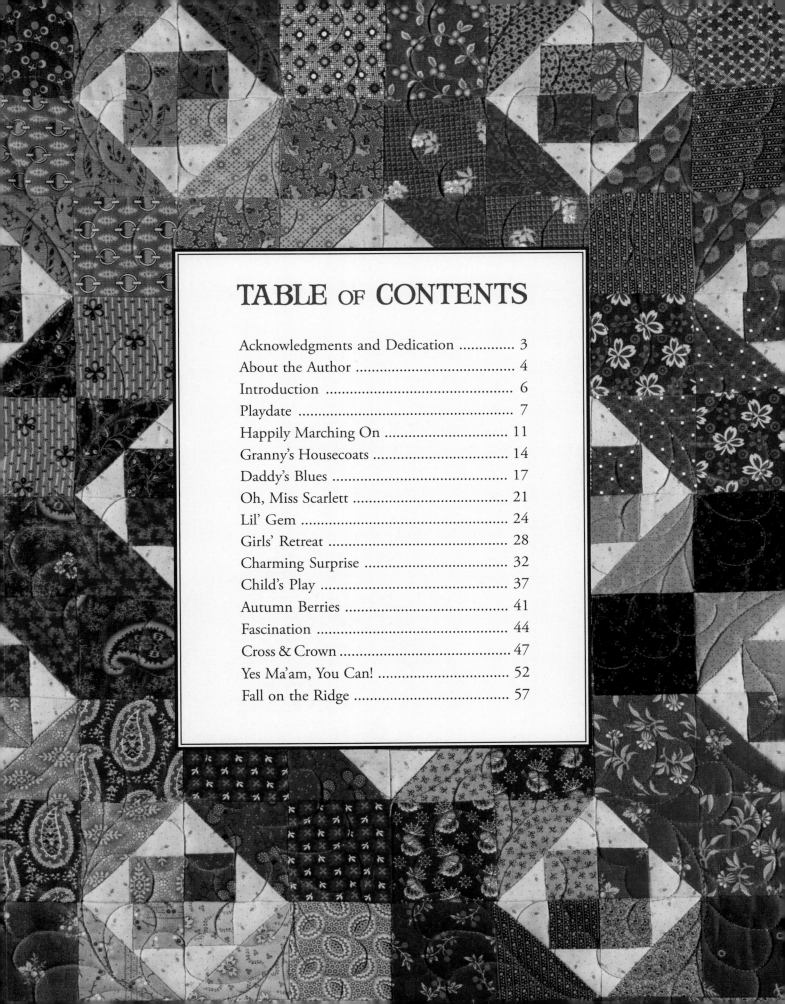

TABLE OF CONTENTS

INTRODUCTION

From the fabrics I purchase to the scraps I receive in the mail from fellow quilters trying to de-clutter their sewing rooms, my stash of fabrics is ever growing. One of my overflowing scrap fabric boxes needed to be tamed. As I sifted through that lovely box of leftover 5" charm squares, I knew I could not be the only person on earth who had such remnants from other projects. This thought sparked one of those light-bulb moments—Why not see what little treasures I could make with those bits and pieces of fabric? This book is the result of those efforts. I worked solely from my box of leftovers and swapped charm squares with fellow quilters and fabric lovers. The only fabrics needed for the featured quilts that are larger than the scraps I used are for the setting elements, border, binding, and backing (NOTE: The blocks in the *Autumn Berries* project on page 41 require 6" squares instead of 5" charm squares).

The idea for this book also stems from my love of scrappy quilts and little quilts. By combining those two favorites of mine and through many late-night sewing adventures, you hold in your hands the result of a quilter gone wild and still running with scissors. (Sorry, Mom, for breaking that rule!)

Happy quilting,

Tara

PLAYDATE

MADE AND QUILTED BY *Tara Lynn Darr*

FINISHED SIZE: 18" x 21"

PLAYDATE

Simple 2" squares and half-square triangle units made from fabrics in your scrap bag make this little quilt easy and fast to piece. The finished quilt makes a great gift for a friend or a charming focal point in your home. I love to decorate my home with these delightful scrappy treasures. They add a welcome pop of color to tabletop centerpieces or rolled up in crocks and buckets. The ideas are endless!

FABRIC REQUIREMENTS

13 medium/dark print charm squares (5" squares)
31 light print charm squares (5" squares)
22" x 25" fabric of choice for backing
¼ yard tan print for binding

CUTTING INSTRUCTIONS

From *each* of 18 light print charm squares, cut:
• 4—2" squares for a total of 72 squares

From *each* of 13 light print charm squares, cut:
• 4—2⅜" squares for a total of 48 squares

From *each* of 13 medium/dark charm squares, cut:
• 4—2⅜" squares for a total of 48 squares

From tan print, cut:
• 3—2½" strips the width of fabric for binding

Tara's Tips

To make this scrappy quilt even scrappier, dig into your stash and cut each of the required 2" and 2⅜" squares from a different print to make this a true charm quilt instead of cutting all your squares from the fabric requirements above. And don't be picky! Remember that even the ugliest fabrics are beautiful when they are cut small enough!

SEWING INSTRUCTIONS

1. On the wrong side of the 48—2⅜" light print fabric squares, mark a diagonal line from corner to corner with a permanent pen, pencil, or chalk marker.

2. With right sides together, layer a marked 2⅜" light print square on top of a 2⅜" dark print square. Sew a scant ¼" seam allowance from both sides of the drawn line.

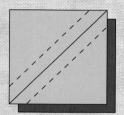

3. Cut the squares apart on the drawn line and press the seams open. You should have a total of 2—2" squares.

4. Repeat steps 2 and 3 to create a total of 96 half-square triangle units.

5. Referring to the quilt assembly diagram on page 10, lay out the 2" light print squares and 96 half-square triangle units in 14 rows of 12 units each. Note that the outermost edge is made with 2" light print squares.

6. Sew together the units within the rows, then join the rows.

7. Sandwich the quilt top, batting, and backing; baste. Quilt as desired, then bind.

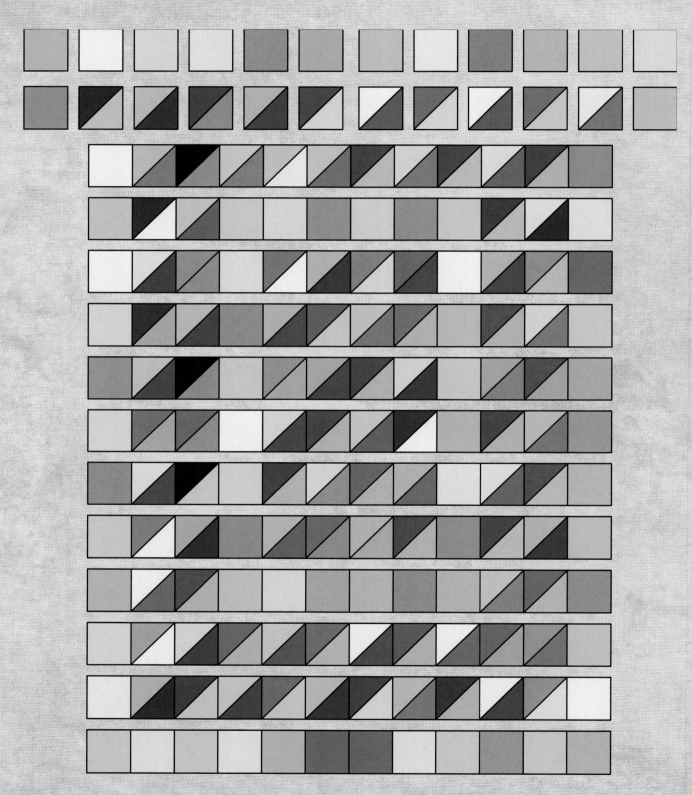

QUILT ASSEMBLY DIAGRAM

HAPPILY MARCHING ON

MADE BY *Tara Lynn Darr*

QUILTED BY *Valerie Langue of The Quilt Merchant*

FINISHED SIZE: 16" x 19"

HAPPILY MARCHING ON

I love the play of colors in this little quilt that gets its name from the movement of the fabrics, which appear to be marching in little stair steps. The colorful steps also serve as a happy reminder to keep marching on throughout life in all that we do.

FABRIC REQUIREMENTS

14 medium/dark print charm squares (5" squares)
14 light print charm squares (5" squares)
20" x 23" fabric of choice for backing
¼ yard dark blue print for binding

CUTTING INSTRUCTIONS

From the 14 light print charm squares, cut:
- 72—1½" x 2½" rectangles
- 8—1½" squares

From the 14 medium/dark print charm squares, cut:
- 72—1½" x 2½" rectangles
- 8—1½" squares

From dark blue print, cut:
- 3—2½" strips the width of fabric for binding

Tara's Tips

When working on these small quilts, become one with your pins. They're so helpful when matching up two seams and holding them together as you sew.

SEWING INSTRUCTIONS

1. Referring to the quilt assembly diagram below, lay out the 8—1½" medium/dark print squares, 72—1½" x 2½" medium/dark print rectangles, 8—1½" light print squares, and 72—1½" x 2½" light print rectangles.

2. Sew together each of the units within the vertical rows, then join the rows.

3. Sandwich the quilt top, batting, and backing; baste. Quilt as desired, then bind.

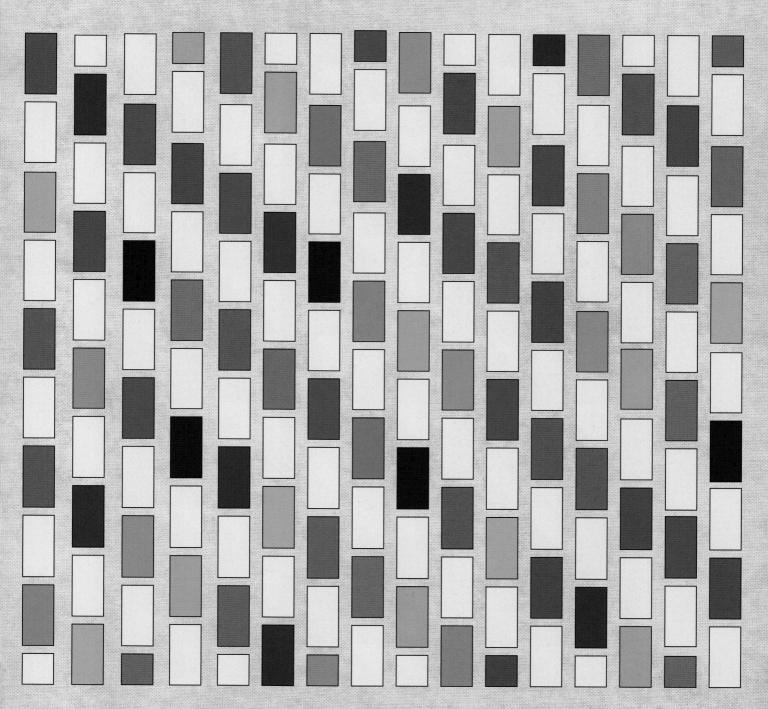

QUILT ASSEMBLY DIAGRAM

GRANNY'S HOUSECOATS

MADE AND QUILTED BY *Tara Lynn Darr*

FINISHED SIZE: 16" X 21"

I have fond childhood memories of my Grandma Lucille's pretty housecoats. Occasionally, I would see her in a dress and on a rare occasion, pants and blouse, but housecoats were her usual attire. It seemed like she had one in every color. Now that Grandma is no longer with us, I treasure those memories of her housecoats even more. I can still remember their beautiful floral patterns and how soft they were, but most of all how beautiful my Grandma looked in them. She made those old housecoats shine. I wish I could have incorporated some of the fabrics from her housecoats into this quilt, but that's okay. I pretended to and that's all that matters to me.

FABRIC REQUIREMENTS

24 medium/dark print charm squares (5" squares) for blocks
24 light print charm squares (5" squares) for blocks
⅛ yard cheddar print for sashing cornerstones
¼ yard black print for sashing
20" x 25" fabric of choice for backing
¼ yard black print for binding

CUTTING INSTRUCTIONS

From light print charm squares, cut:
• 96—1⅞" squares for blocks

From medium/dark print charm squares, cut:
• 96—1⅞" squares for blocks

From cheddar print, cut:
• 20—1½" squares for sashing cornerstones

From black print, cut:
• 31—1½" x 4½" strips for sashing
• 3—2½" strips the width of fabric for binding

SEWING INSTRUCTIONS

1. On the wrong side of the 96—1⅞" light print squares, mark a diagonal line from corner to corner with a permanent pen, pencil, or chalk marker.

2. With right sides together, layer a marked 1⅞" light print square on top of a 1⅞" medium/dark print square. Sew a scant ¼" seam allowance from both sides of the drawn line.

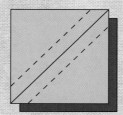

3. Cut the squares apart on the drawn line and press the seams open to yield a total of 2—1½" squares.

4. Repeat steps 2 and 3 to create a total of 192 half-square triangle units.

5. Sew together 16 half-square triangle units to create a block. Repeat to create a total of 12—4½" square blocks.

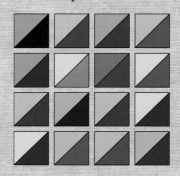

6. Referring to the quilt assembly diagram below, lay out the 12 blocks from step 5, the 31 black print sashing strips, and the 20—1½" square cheddar print sashing cornerstones.

7. Referring to the quilt assembly diagram, sew together the units from step 6 to complete the quilt top.

8. Sandwich the quilt top, batting, and backing; baste. Quilt as desired, then bind.

QUILT ASSEMBLY DIAGRAM

DADDY'S BLUES

MADE AND QUILTED BY *Tara Lynn Darr*

FINISHED SIZE: 19" X 23½"

DADDY'S BLUES

This little quilt's name reflects my husband's love of the color blue. When he sees one of my quilts and says that "it plays with my eyes," it usually means that pattern will be a winner. We'll see if that holds true for some of the patterns in this book as well!

FABRIC REQUIREMENTS

16 medium/dark print charm squares (5" squares) for blocks
16 light print charm squares (5" squares) for blocks
⅛ yard light print for setting squares
⅛ yard medium blue print for setting squares
⅜ yard dark blue print for setting triangles and corner triangles
22" x 26" fabric of choice for backing
¼ yard dark blue print for binding

CUTTING INSTRUCTIONS

*Please note that some of the Nine-Patches in Tara's quilt are "positive," meaning that they use five squares of dark fabric and four squares of light fabric, while others are "negative," meaning that they use five squares of light fabric and four squares of dark fabric. Tara's quilt includes 11 positive Nine-Patches and nine negative Nine-Patches. She used just two fabrics per Nine-Patch but you can make them scrappier by using more fabrics than that. Plenty of charm square fabric was listed in the **Fabric Requirements** if you want to switch the number of positive and negative Nine-Patches or if you want to make scrappy Nine-Patches.*

From *each* of 11 medium/dark print charm squares, cut:
• 5—1½" squares for Nine-Patches

From *each* of nine medium/dark print charm squares, cut:
• 4—1½" squares for Nine-Patches

From *each* of 11 light print charm squares, cut:
• 4—1½" squares for Nine-Patches

From *each* of nine light print charm squares, cut:
• 5—1½" squares for Nine-Patches

From light print, cut:
• 4—3½" squares for setting squares

From medium blue print, cut:
• 8—3½" squares for setting squares

From dark blue print, cut:
• 4—8½" squares, then cut those squares in half diagonally twice for a total of 14 setting triangles
• 2—4½" squares, then cut those squares in half diagonally once for a total of four corner triangles
• 3—2½" strips the width of fabric for binding

SEWING INSTRUCTIONS

1. Using 5—1½" medium/dark print squares and 4—1½" light print squares, make a positive Nine-Patch. Repeat to make a total of 11 positive Nine-Patches.

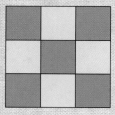

2. Using 4—1½" medium/dark print squares and 5—1½" light print squares, make a negative Nine-Patch. Repeat to make a total of nine negative Nine-Patches.

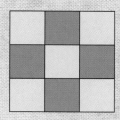

3. Referring to the quilt assembly diagram on page 20, lay out the 20 Nine-Patches, 8—3½" medium blue print setting squares, 4—3½" light print setting squares, 14 dark blue print setting triangles, and four dark blue corner triangles.

4. Referring to the quilt assembly diagram, sew together the units from step 3 to complete the quilt top.
NOTE: The dark blue setting triangles are oversized to create a floating effect for the Nine-Patch blocks, which do not touch the edge of the quilt.

5. Sandwich the quilt top, batting, and backing; baste. Quilt as desired, then bind.

QUILT ASSEMBLY DIAGRAM

OH, MISS SCARLETT

MADE BY *Tara Lynn Darr*

QUILTED BY *Valerie Langue of The Quilt Merchant*

FINISHED SIZE: 15" X 15"

OH, MISS SCARLETT

I was named after a famous fictional plantation in Georgia. When my Mom and Dad were dating, they went to see the movie, "Gone with the Wind," twice. To this day, Mom still loves it. My brother was almost named after the main male character in the movie but alas, it wasn't meant to be. However, our family did get an "Ashley" when I named my daughter after him!

FABRIC REQUIREMENTS

36 red print charm squares (5" squares) for blocks
36 light print charm squares (5" squares) for blocks
19" x 19" fabric of choice for backing
¼ yard red print for binding

CUTTING INSTRUCTIONS

The template on page 23 does not include a seam allowance. Depending on your preferred appliqué method, you may need to add a seam allowance to it.

From light print charm squares, cut:
• 18—3½" squares for block backgrounds
• 18 of Template A for melon shapes

From red print charm squares, cut:
• 18—3½" squares for block backgrounds
• 18 of Template A for melon shapes

From red print, cut:
• 2—2½" strips the width of fabric for binding

SEWING INSTRUCTIONS

1. Using your preferred appliqué method and referring to the diagrams below for placement, appliqué each of the melon shapes to a 3½" square, noting that Tara made 18 blocks with a light melon shape on a red square and 18 blocks with a red melon shape on a light square. Be sure to center the melons on the blocks to accommodate a ¼" seam allowance. Press the blocks, then trim them to measure 3" square.

2. Referring to the quilt assembly diagram below, lay out the 36 blocks from step 1, then sew them together to complete the quilt top.

3. Sandwich the quilt top, batting, and backing; baste. Quilt as desired, then bind.

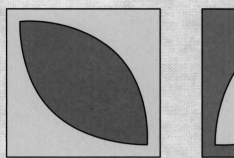

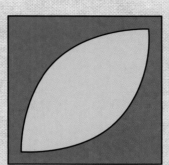

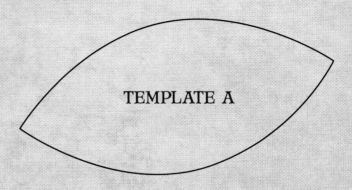

Template does NOT include a seam allowance

QUILT ASSEMBLY DIAGRAM

LIL' GEM

MADE BY *Tara Lynn Darr*
QUILTED BY *Valerie Langue of The Quilt Merchant*

FINISHED SIZE: 14" x 14"

I've said it before, but I like to repeat myself just like some of my favorite fabrics tend to repeat themselves in my quilts—Use your scrap bags! If you don't have one, start one today and stop throwing away all those bits of fabric that you think are too small or that you'll never use. They are the perfect picks for little quilts like this one.

FABRIC REQUIREMENTS

1 red print charm square (5" square) for center block
2 charm squares (5" squares) in different red print than above for center block
2 black print charm squares (5" squares) for center block
1 light print charm square (5" square) for center block
3 charm squares (5" squares) in different light print than above for center block
40 assorted medium/dark print charm squares for quarter-square triangle unit border
18" square fabric of choice for backing
¼ yard black print for binding

CUTTING INSTRUCTIONS

From red print charm square, cut:
•1—2½" square (A) for center block

From one light print charm square, cut:
• 1—3¼" square, then cut the square in half diagonally twice (B) for center block

From two black print charm squares, cut:
• 2—3¼" squares, then cut those squares in half diagonally twice (C) for center block

From the remaining three light print charm squares, cut:
• 1—3¼" square, then cut the square in half diagonally twice (D) for center block
• 2—2⅞" squares, then cut those squares in half diagonally once (E) for center block

From the remaining two red print squares, cut:
• 2—2⅞" squares, then cut those squares in half diagonally once (F) for center block

From assorted medium/dark print charm squares, cut:
• 40—3¼" squares, then cut those squares in half diagonally twice for the quarter-square triangle-unit border

From black print, cut:
• 3—2½" strips the width of fabric for binding

Tara's Tips

Do you have one of those handy 2½" square little charm collections available at quilt shops that are so popular today? They are a great resource for making the kind of quilts featured in this book, especially if you haven't yet amassed a good stash of scraps!

SEWING INSTRUCTIONS

Center Star Block

1. Sew together the C, B, and D triangles to create a total of four quarter-square triangle units. Press the seams open.

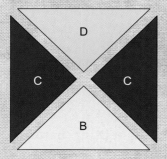 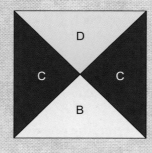

2. Sew together the F and E triangles to create a total of four half-square triangle units. Press the seams open.

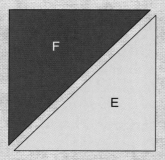 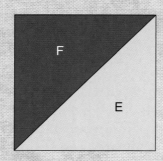

3. Sew together the units from steps 1 and 2 and a 2½" red print square (A) to complete the center block. Press all the seams open.

Quarter-Square Triangle Unit Border

1. Sew together four different medium/dark triangles to create a quarter-square triangle unit. To reduce bulk, press the seams open. Repeat to create a total of 40 quarter-square triangle units.

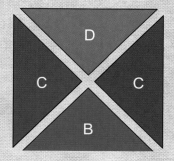 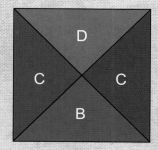

2. Sew together 14 quarter-square triangle units to create a top border. Repeat to create a bottom border.

3. Sew together six quarter-square triangle units to create a side border. Repeat to create a second side border.

Completing the Quilt

1. Referring to the quilt assembly diagram below, sew the side borders to the center star block.

2. Referring to the quilt assembly diagram, sew the top and bottom borders to the quilt top.

3. Sandwich the quilt top, batting, and backing; baste. Quilt as desired, then bind.

QUILT ASSEMBLY DIAGRAM

GIRLS' RETREAT

MADE BY *Tara Lynn Darr*

QUILTED BY *Valerie Langue of The Quilt Merchant*

FINISHED SIZE: 15" x 17"

Quilting retreats are so much fun. The special bonding time with girlfriends and the sharing of thoughts, treasured secrets, and our future hopes and wishes are priceless moments. I also appreciate the creative energy and honest feedback on my projects from fellow quilters. After I made this quilt, I thought of each of its small Xes as representations of hugs. At the end of every retreat I attend, I like to give each of my special quilting friends a hug with the promise of getting together for future retreats.

FABRIC REQUIREMENTS

42 medium/dark print charm squares (5" squares)
20 light print charm squares (5" squares)
19" x 21" fabric of choice for backing
¼ yard dark blue print for binding

CUTTING INSTRUCTIONS

To stay organized for sewing, Tara keeps the matching medium/dark print rectangles and squares (listed below) for the blocks in sets. You should have a total of 42 sets.

From light print charm squares, cut:
• 153—1½" squares for blocks, setting triangles, and three corner triangles

From *each* of the medium/dark print charm squares, cut:
• 1—1½" x 3½" rectangle for blocks
• 2—1½" squares for blocks and one corner square

From dark blue print, cut:
• 3—2½" strips the width of fabric for binding

Tara's Tips

A design board comes in handy for quilts with lots of little pieces like this one. If you do not have a design board, you can easily create your own with an inexpensive flannel-backed tablecloth available at dollar stores. The tablecloth is also easy to roll up and move out of the way if needed.

SEWING INSTRUCTIONS

1. Using the same medium/dark print squares and rectangle and four different light print squares for each block, sew together 2—1½" medium/dark print squares, 4—1½" light print squares, and 1—1½" x 3½" medium/dark print rectangle to create one block. Repeat to create a total of 21 blocks.

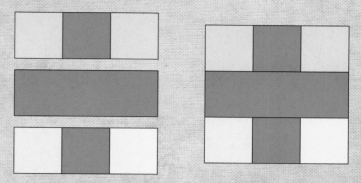

2. Referring to the quilt assembly diagram below, lay out the 21 blocks from step 1, 21—1½" x 3½" medium/dark print sashing strips, 29 sashing cornerstones and corner squares, and 11 setting "triangles." (Each setting "triangle" is made of 2—1½" light print squares and 1—1½" medium/dark print square.)

3. Sew the units in step 2 into rows, then join the rows to complete the quilt top.

4. Sandwich the quilt top, batting, and backing; baste. Quilt as desired. Tara simply squared the quilt up by cutting off the jagged edges, shown in the following diagram, leaving a ¼" seam allowance around the points of the Xes to attach the binding without cutting off their points.

5. Bind the quilt.

QUILT ASSEMBLY DIAGRAM

CHARMING SURPRISE

MADE BY *Tara Lynn Darr*

QUILTED BY *Valerie Langue of The Quilt Merchant*

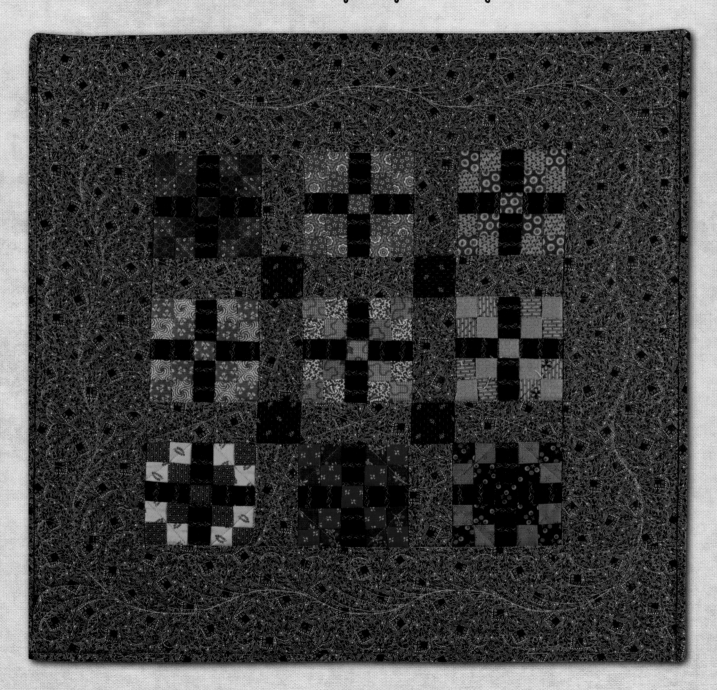

FINISHED SIZE: 29" X 29"

I created this quilt while on a personal quilting retreat at a fellow quilting friend's home. While she was away, she granted me full use of her lovely studio where I could create to my heart's content. I worked late in the night and rose with the sun to enjoy a peaceful morning, drinking coffee and enjoying her gardens. This quilt is special to me because I bought many of its fabrics at the local quilt shop, which is also owned by the sweet friend who graciously allowed me to use her studio. But the border fabric is another story. It is one of those fabrics that didn't play nicely with a lot of other fabrics, however, I was determined to find a project for it. Late at night while making all the Four-Patches for this quilt at my friend's house, the featured border fabric popped into my head. I had packed it in the bins of fabrics and supplies in my car, so I traipsed outside in my jammies with a flashlight in hand and dug through the bins to find it. Needless to say, I'll bet the neighbors thought I was a nut!

FABRIC REQUIREMENTS

18 medium/dark print charm squares (5" squares) for blocks
¼ yard black with small print for blocks and sashing cornerstones
⅞ yard gray/black print for sashing, border, and binding
33" square fabric of choice for backing

CUTTING INSTRUCTIONS

Each of the nine blocks contains four Four-Patch units. To make them, Tara first selects which two medium/dark print charm squares she wants to use for each unit and pairs them before cutting the charm squares to the necessary sizes listed below. To stay organized for sewing the Four-Patch units together, she keeps the cut fabrics for each block separated into sets.

From *each* of nine medium/dark print charm squares, cut:
• 9—1½" squares for blocks

From *each* of nine medium/dark print charm squares, cut:
• 8—1½" squares for blocks

From black with small print, cut:
• 36—1½" x 2½" strips for blocks
• 4—2½" squares for sashing cornerstones

From gray/black print, cut:
• 12—2½" x 5½" strips for sashing
• 2—5½" x 19½" strips for side borders
• 2—5½" x 29½" strips for top and bottom borders
• 3—2½" strips the width of fabric for binding

Tara's Tips

Put those odd fabrics you don't know what to do with to good use in your border and setting fabrics. The fabric I chose for this quilt's borders and sashing didn't go well with a lot of fabrics in my previous projects, but I loved it in this project. Luckily, it turned out to be the perfect pick for this quilt's border because it complements the simple black print in the blocks.

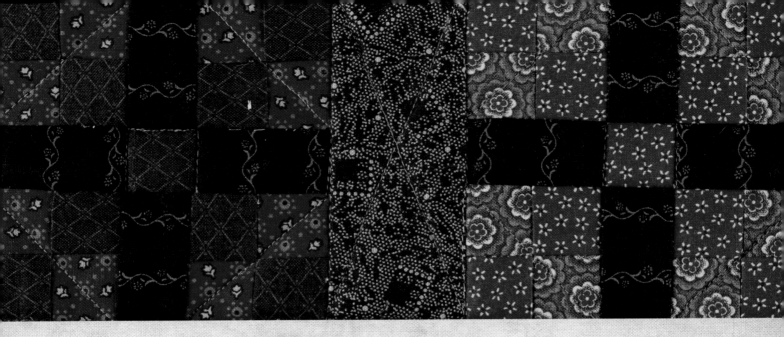

Blocks

1. Sew together 2—1½" squares of one medium/dark print and 2—1½" squares of a different medium/dark print to create a Four-Patch. Repeat to create a total of four Four-Patches using those same fabric combinations. To reduce bulk, press the seams open.

2. Sew together four matching Four-Patches, 4—1½" x 2½" black with small print strips, and a 1½" medium/dark print square to complete a block. Press the seams toward the black strips. Repeat to create a total of nine blocks.

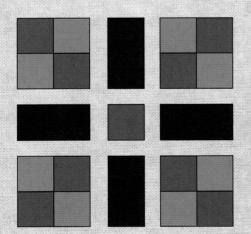

Sashing

Sew together 3—2½" x 5½" gray/black print strips and 2—2½" black with small print squares to create a sashing strip. Repeat to create a second sashing strip.

Quilt Assembly

1. Referring to the following diagram, sew together the three blocks and 2—2½" x 5½" gray/black print strips to create a row. Repeat to create three rows. Then sew together the three block rows from this step and the two sashing strips from the previous section to complete the quilt center.

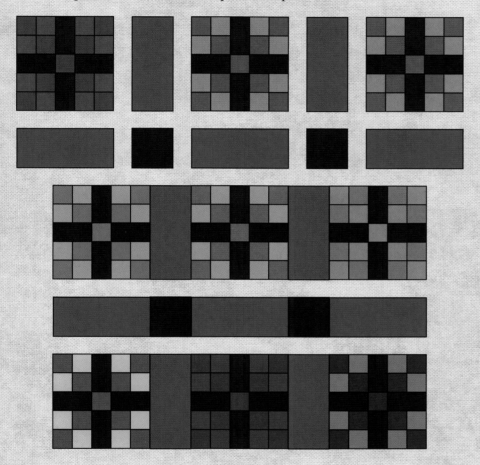

2. Referring to the quilt assembly diagram on page 36, sew the gray/black print side border strips to the quilt center.

3. Referring to the quilt assembly diagram, sew the gray/black print top and bottom borders to the quilt top.

4. Sandwich the quilt top, batting, and backing; baste. Quilt as desired, then bind.

QUILT ASSEMBLY DIAGRAM

CHILD'S PLAY

MADE BY *Tara Lynn Darr*
QUILTED BY *Valerie Langue of The Quilt Merchant*

FINISHED SIZE: 16" X 24"

CHILD'S PLAY

Do you remember playing with a fresh box of crayons as a child? I loved the beginning of the school year when I got a big box of crayons. I have such sweet memories of dumping them out on the floor, then matching up the colors I liked. Playing with fabric is a lot like that for me—I pull colors from my shelves and scrap bins like a child with her crayons. Before long, there are colorful piles of fabric everywhere. Let your inner child play with colors to create your own perfect quilt!

FABRIC REQUIREMENTS

48 medium/dark print charm squares (5" squares)
   for blocks
⅛ yard cream print for blocks
20" x 28" fabric of choice for backing
¼ yard brown print for binding

CUTTING INSTRUCTIONS

Each of the blocks (shown below) is made of two squares of the same color in addition to two units made of one large triangle, two small triangles, and one square. For each of the latter two units, Tara used two different medium/dark prints. To stay organized for sewing the blocks together later, she pairs the two different colored medium/dark print charm squares before cutting the charm squares to the necessary sizes in the cutting list, then keeps the cut fabrics for each block separated into sets.

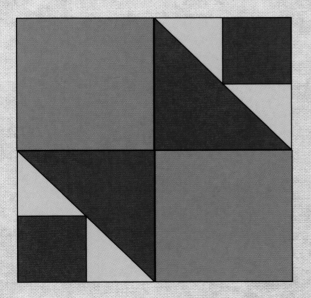

From *each* of 24 medium/dark print charm squares, cut:
• 2—1½" squares for blocks
• 1—2⅞" square, then cut the square in half diagonally once to make a total of two triangles for blocks

From *each* of 24 medium/dark print charm squares, cut:
• 2—2½" squares for blocks

From cream print, cut:
• 48—1⅞" squares, then cut each of the squares in half diagonally once to make a total of 96 triangles for blocks

From brown print, cut:
• 3—2½" strips the width of fabric for binding

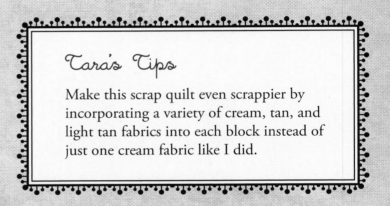

Tara's Tips

Make this scrap quilt even scrappier by incorporating a variety of cream, tan, and light tan fabrics into each block instead of just one cream fabric like I did.

SEWING INSTRUCTIONS

1. With right sides together, layer a cream print triangle on top of a 1½" medium/dark print square. Press the seam toward the triangle.

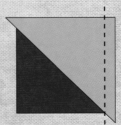

2. Sew another cream print triangle to the unit from step 1. Press the seam toward the triangle. Clip the "dog-ears" where the two triangles meet.

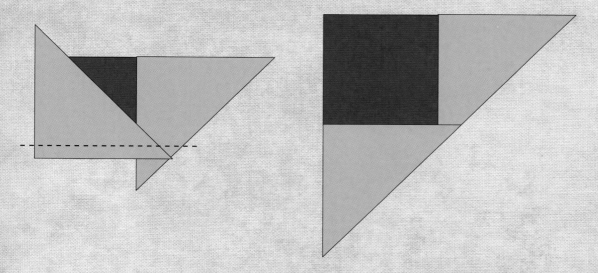

3. Sew a large triangle that matches the color of the medium/dark print square in the unit from step 2 to the unit from step 2.

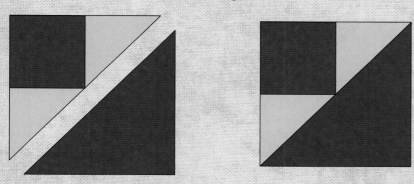

4. Repeat steps 1—3 to create another unit like the one in step 3.

5. Sew together the two units from steps 3 and 4 to 2—2½" medium/dark print squares to create a block. To reduce bulk, press the seams open.

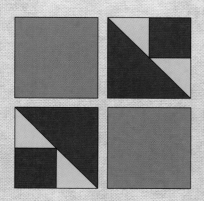
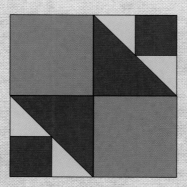

6. Repeat steps 1—5 to create a total of 24 blocks.

7. Referring to the quilt assembly diagram below, sew together the 24 blocks into rows, then join the rows. To create the necessary design, be careful to position the blocks so the units containing a large triangle, two small triangles, and a square abut with the same type of units in other blocks. Press the seams in the rows in opposite directions.

8. Sandwich the quilt top, batting, and backing; baste. Quilt as desired, then bind.

QUILT ASSEMBLY DIAGRAM

AUTUMN BERRIES

MADE BY *Tara Lynn Darr*

QUILTED BY *Valerie Langue of The Quilt Merchant*

FINISHED SIZE: 18" x 18"

AUTUMN BERRIES

I love all of autumn's sensory delights—the smell of the crisp air, the colors of falling leaves, and the sounds of chirping birds and squirrels gathering nuts. For this quilt, I was inspired by autumn's beautiful palette of deep reds, rich browns, and mellow tans. While designing it, I pulled out photos of autumn travels I had taken and revisited many sweet memories.

FABRIC REQUIREMENTS

11 red print 6" squares for blocks
11 brown print 6" squares for blocks
10 tan print 6" squares for blocks
⅓ yard black paisley for border
22" square fabric of choice for backing
¼ yard dark brown paisley for binding

CUTTING INSTRUCTIONS

Each of the 16 blocks are made of two different prints. To make them, Tara pairs two different colored 6" squares before cutting them to the necessary sizes listed below. To stay organized for sewing, she keeps each of the cut fabrics for each block separated into sets.

From *each* of 16 red, brown, and tan squares, cut:
• 3—1⅞" squares, then cut those squares in half diagonally once to create a total of six triangles for blocks

From *each* of the remaining 16 red, brown, and tan squares, cut:
• 3—1½" squares for blocks
• 3—1⅞" squares, then cut those squares in half diagonally once to create a total of six triangles for blocks

From dark brown paisley, cut:
• 2—3½" x 12½" strips for side borders
• 2—3½" x 18½" strips for top and bottom borders
• 3—2½" strips the width of fabric for binding

SEWING INSTRUCTIONS

1. Using the fabric sets you set aside earlier, sew together two different colored triangles with right sides together to create a half-square triangle unit. Press the seam toward the darker fabric. Repeat to create a total of six half-square triangle units.

2. Sew together three 1½" squares and six half-square triangle units from step 1 to create a block. Press the seams in the top and bottom rows toward the two outer units and press the seams in the middle row toward the center square. To reduce bulk, press the seams that join the rows open.

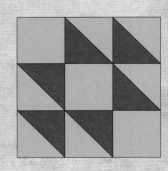

3. Repeat steps 1 and 2 to create a total of 16 blocks.

4. Referring to the quilt assembly diagram below, lay out the 16 blocks from step 3.

5. Referring to the quilt assembly diagram, sew together the 16 blocks to create the quilt center. In each row, press the seams in opposite directions. To reduce bulk, press the seams that join the rows open.

6. Referring to the quilt assembly diagram, sew the black paisley side borders to the quilt center, then sew the top and bottom borders to the quilt top. Press the seams toward the border.

7. Sandwich the quilt top, batting, and backing; baste. Quilt as desired, then bind.

QUILT ASSEMBLY DIAGRAM

FASCINATION

MADE BY *Tara Lynn Darr*
QUILTED BY *Valerie Langue of The Quilt Merchant*

FINISHED SIZE: 18 ¾" X 23"

Like many quilters, I am fascinated by star patterns. A charming galaxy of traditional star blocks twinkles against a neutral backdrop in this little quilt made from charm squares.

FABRIC REQUIREMENTS

12 medium/dark print charm squares (5" squares) for star blocks
12 assorted light print charm squares (5" squares) for star blocks
⅓ yard light tan print for setting blocks
¼ yard dark brown print for setting triangles
23" x 27" fabric of choice for backing
¼ yard dark brown print for binding

Tara's Tips

When sewing the star blocks for this quilt, make sure you have a fresh, sharp needle in your sewing machine and slow the speed of your machine. For best results, use pins as you stitch to hold the segments together. I also like to use a finer 50- or 60-weight thread because less thread bulk in the seams makes it easier to achieve a more accurate seam allowance.

CUTTING INSTRUCTIONS

For each of the star blocks, Tara used the same fabric for the star points. Keep that in mind when cutting the 2¼" medium/dark squares below, which are used for the star points, and be sure that the 2" medium/dark squares you select coordinate with the corresponding star points.

From *each* of the medium/dark charm squares, cut:
• 1—2" square for star blocks
• 2—2¼" squares, then cut those squares in half diagonally twice to create a total of 96 triangles for star points

From assorted light charm squares, cut:
• 12—2¼" squares, then cut those squares in half diagonally twice to create a total of 48 triangles for star blocks
• 48—1½" squares for star blocks

From light tan print, cut:
• 20—3½" squares for setting blocks

From dark brown print, cut:
• 4—7" squares, then cut those squares in half diagonally twice to create a total of 16 setting triangles (you will only need 14 of them)
• 2—3¾" squares, then cut those squares in half diagonally once to create a total of four corner triangles
• 3—2½" strips the width of fabric for binding

SEWING INSTRUCTIONS

1. Referring to the following diagram, sew together 4—1½" light print squares, four light print triangles, eight medium/dark print triangles, and one 2" medium/dark print square to complete a star block. Repeat to create a total of 12 blocks.

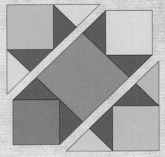 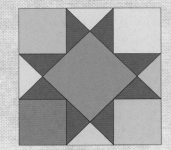

2. Referring the quilt assembly diagram below, lay out the 12 star blocks, 20—3½" light tan print square setting blocks, 14 dark brown setting triangles, and four dark brown corner triangles. Sew those units together to complete the quilt top. **NOTE:** the brown setting triangles are oversized to create a floating effect for the blocks, which do not touch the edge of the quilt.

3. Sandwich the quilt top, batting, and backing; baste. Quilt as desired, then bind.

QUILT ASSEMBLY DIAGRAM

CROSS & CROWN

PIECED AND HAND QUILTED BY *Tara Lynn Darr*

FINISHED SIZE: 25" X 32½"

CROSS & CROWN

Don't let this traditional block intimidate you. It looks harder than it actually is. I made my blocks scrappy by incorporating multiple blue, brown, and cream prints instead of just one of each. The quilt's warm tones create an inviting display for practically any room. Mine has a happy home in my living room.

FABRIC REQUIREMENTS

4 assorted brown print charm squares (5" squares) for blocks
12 assorted blue print charm squares (5" squares) for blocks
14 assorted cream print charm squares (5" squares) for blocks
¼ yard brown print for first border
½ yard tan print for setting squares, setting triangles, corner triangles, and middle border
¾ yard dark blue print for outer border and binding
29" x 36" fabric of choice for backing

Tara's Tips

The open areas in this quilt's setting blocks and outer border are the perfect places to practice your hand quilting. I find this type of quilting very relaxing. Give it a try. You just might discover a new passion!

CUTTING INSTRUCTIONS

To create a scrappy look, Tara used multiple blue, brown, and cream prints instead of just one of each for her blocks. To create a similar look, keep that in mind as you cut your brown, blue, and cream prints below for the blocks.

From brown print charm squares, cut:
• 12—2¼" squares for blocks

From blue print charm squares, cut:
• 6—1½" squares for blocks
• 12—2⅞" squares, then cut those squares in half diagonally once for a total of 24 triangles for blocks

From cream print charm squares, cut:
• 24—1½" squares for blocks
• 12—2¼" squares for blocks
• 24—1½" x 2½" rectangles for blocks

From tan print, cut:
• 2—5½" squares for setting blocks
• 2—11⅞" squares, then cut those squares in half diagonally twice for a total of six setting triangles (you will only need four of them)
• 2—6⅛" squares, then cut those squares in half diagonally once for a total of four corner triangles
• 2—1" x 25½" strips for middle side borders
• 2—1" x 19½" strips for middle top and bottom borders

From brown print, cut:
• 2—1½" x 23½" strips for first side borders
• 2—1½" x 18½" strips for first top and bottom borders

From dark blue print, cut:
• 2—3½" x 26½" strips for outer side borders
• 2—3½" x 25½" strips for outer top and bottom borders

From blue print, cut:
• 4—2½" strips the width of fabric for binding

SEWING INSTRUCTIONS

Blocks

1. On the wrong side of all the 12—2¼" cream print squares, mark a diagonal line from corner to corner with a permanent pen, pencil, or chalk marker.

2. Layer a marked cream print square on top of a 2¼" brown print square. Then sew a scant ¼" seam allowance from both sides of the drawn line.

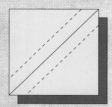

3. Cut the square apart on the drawn line, then press the seams open to yield a total of 2—1⅞" half-square triangle units.

4. Repeat steps 2–3 to create a total of 24 half-square triangle units.

5. Referring to the following diagram, cut each of the 24 half-square triangle units in half to create a total of 48 triangles.

6. Sew a 1½" cream print square to a triangle from step 5 in which the smaller brown triangle is on the left. Press the seams open.

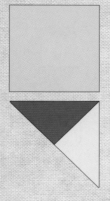

7. Sew a pieced triangle in which the smaller brown triangle is on the right to the unit from step 6. Press the seams open.

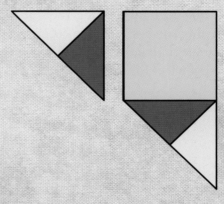

8. Sew a blue print triangle cut from the 2⅞" blue print squares to the unit from step 7.

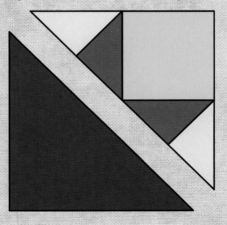

9. Repeat steps 6–8 to create a total of 24 units like the one in step 8. Press the seams open.

10. Referring to the following diagram, sew together four units from step 9, four 1½" x 2½" cream print rectangles, and one 1½" blue print square to complete a block. Press the seams open or to opposite sides so that the seams lock together. Repeat to create a total of 6—5½" square blocks.

Quilt Assembly

1. Referring to the following diagram, sew together the six blocks from step 10 on this page, the two medium print setting squares, the six medium print setting triangles, and the four medium print corner triangles to complete the quilt center. **NOTE:** the setting triangles are oversized to create a floating effect for the blocks, which do not touch the first border.

2. Trim the quilt center to measure 16½" x 23½".

3. Referring to the quilt assembly diagram below, sew the first brown border's side strips to the quilt center. Press the seams toward the border. Sew the first border's top and bottom strips to the quilt top. Press the seams toward the border.

4. Referring to the quilt assembly diagram, sew the middle tan border side strips to the sides of the quilt top. Press the seams toward the outermost border. Sew the middle tan border's top and bottom strips to the quilt top. Press the seams toward the outermost border.

5. Referring to the quilt assembly diagram, sew the outer blue print border side strips to the sides of the quilt top. Press the seams toward the outer border. Sew the outer blue print border top and bottom strips to the quilt top. Press the seams toward the outer border.

6. Sandwich the quilt top, batting, and backing; baste. Quilt as desired, then bind.

QUILT ASSEMBLY DIAGRAM

YES MA'AM, YOU CAN!

PIECED AND HAND QUILTED BY *Tara Lynn Darr*

FINISHED SIZE: 34½" x 36½"

Yes ma'am, it's time to use up those scraps! Dig into your baskets, boxes, and bins of leftover bits and pieces and you're sure to find good candidates for this strippy quilt.

FABRIC REQUIREMENTS

60–75 medium/dark print charm squares (5" squares) for center patchwork and Flying Geese units
¼ yard light print for Flying Geese units
⅜ yard brown print for border
38" x 40" fabric of choice for backing
⅓ yard different brown print than above for binding

CUTTING INSTRUCTIONS

The Flying Geese units in Tara's quilt feature two different fabrics. If you wish to make them scrappier, you can mix and match the "wing" fabrics by using two different prints rather than one as Tara did. To stay organized for sewing later, Tara separates the cut fabrics for each Flying Geese unit into sets.

From *each* of 28 medium/dark print charm squares, cut:
• 2—2½" squares for Flying Geese units

From light print, cut:
• 28—2½" x 4½" rectangles for Flying Geese units

From the remaining 32–47 medium/dark print charm squares, cut:
• Enough 3"-wide strips of various lengths to create 11—2½" x 28½" strips (Tara used lengths of ¾"–2½")

From brown print, cut:
• 2—2½" x 28½" strips for side borders
• 2—4½" x 34½" strips for top and bottom borders

From brown print 2, cut:
• 4—2½" strips the width of fabric for binding

SEWING INSTRUCTIONS

Quilt Center
1. With right sides together, sew together enough medium/dark print strips along their 3"-long sides to create a row that is at least 28½" long. Don't worry if your row is a bit longer than that as you can trim it to size later. When sewing, Tara grabs her strips from a basket without looking. She doesn't worry if the colors match each other. Press the seams in the same direction. Trim the row to measure 2½" x 28½". Repeat to create a total of 11 strippy rows.

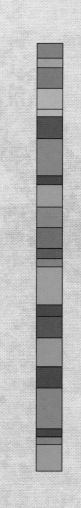

Tara's Tips

Strip-piecing this project's many strips will make faster work of the quilt center.

2. Referring to the following diagram, sew together the 11 strippy rows from step 1 to create the quilt center.

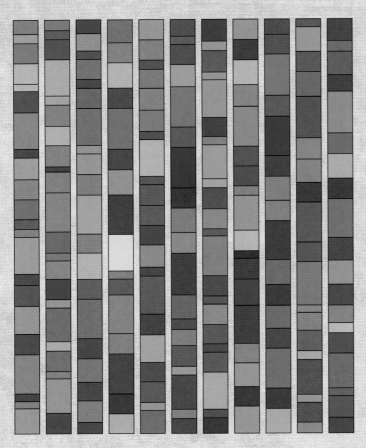

Flying Geese Border

1. On the wrong side of 56—2½" medium/dark print squares, draw a diagonal line from corner to corner with a permanent pen, pencil, or chalk marker.

2. Layer a marked 2½" medium/dark print square on top of a 2½" x 4½" light print rectangle. Sew on the marked line, then trim a ¼" seam allowance from the stitched line and press open the resulting triangle.

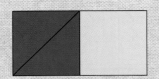 

3. Layer a marked 2½" medium/dark print square on the opposite side of the 2½" x 4½" light print rectangle from the previous step. Sew on the marked line, then trim a ¼" seam allowance from the stitched line and press open the resulting triangle.

4. Repeat steps 2–3 to create a total of 28 Flying Geese units.

5. Referring to the following diagram, sew together 14 Flying Geese units to create a side border strip. Repeat to create a total of two side border strips.

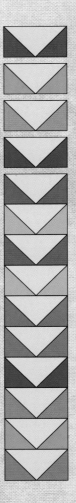

Quilt Assembly

1. Referring to the following diagram, sew the two Flying Geese side border strips to the quilt center.

2. Referring to the quilt assembly diagram on page 56, sew the 2—2½" x 28½" brown print strips to the sides of the quilt top.

3. Referring to the quilt assembly diagram, sew the 2—4½" x 34½" brown print strips to the top and bottom of the quilt top.

4. Sandwich the quilt top, batting, and backing; baste. Quilt as desired, then bind.

QUILT ASSEMBLY DIAGRAM

FALL ON THE RIDGE

MADE BY *Tara Lynn Darr*

QUILTED BY *Valerie Langue of The Quilt Merchant*

FINISHED SIZE: 19" X 19"

FALL ON THE RIDGE

While stitching this quilt, I thought of the beauty of West Virginia's Newsome Ridge where we enjoy taking our four-wheeler on long rides along the trails and forgotten paths. My favorite time of year to ride the ridge is fall when you can see Mother Nature work her colorful magic on the leaves as they change to a pretty palette of red, orange, and rust against the wide open sky and majestic mountains. This quilt's autumnal color scheme recalls those breathtaking rides on the ridge.

FABRIC REQUIREMENTS

16 assorted medium/dark print charm squares (5" squares) for Center block, Flying Geese blocks, and Square blocks

24 assorted light print charm squares (5" squares) for Center block, Flying Geese blocks, Square blocks, and outer setting blocks

4—3½" x 6½" assorted light print rectangles for outer setting blocks

2—14" squares different light print than above for corner setting triangles

23" square fabric of choice for backing

¼ yard cream print for binding

CUTTING INSTRUCTIONS

To stay organized for sewing later, Tara separates some of the fabrics into three categories—Center block, Flying Geese blocks, and Square blocks.

CENTER BLOCK

SQUARE BLOCK

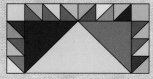

FLYING GEESE BLOCK

From medium/dark prints, cut:
- 1—2¾" square for Center block
- 12—3⅛" squares, then cut those squares in half diagonally once for a total of 24 triangles for Center block and Flying Geese blocks (To stay organized, Tara labels 16 of these "Flying Geese blocks" and four of them "Square blocks".)
- 74—1⅝" squares for half-square triangle units in Flying Geese blocks and Square blocks

From light prints, cut:
- 2—2½" squares, then cut squares in half diagonally once for a total of four triangles for Center block (Tara used two different fabrics for this.)
- 2—3⅛" squares, then cut squares in half diagonally once for a total of four triangles for Square blocks
- 74—1⅝" squares for Flying Geese blocks and Square blocks
- 20—1¼" squares for Flying Geese blocks and Square blocks
- 4—4" squares, then cut squares in half diagonally once for a total of eight triangles for Flying Geese blocks (Tara chose this option to get the variety of prints shown in the featured quilt. If you want to avoid bias edges on the long outer edges of the triangles, you will need to cut 4—7¼" squares, then cut those in half diagonally twice. You will have eight extra triangles with this alternative method.)

From four different light prints, cut:
- 4—3½" x 6½" rectangles for outer setting blocks

From two 14" squares of a different light print than above, cut:
- 2—13⅝" squares, then cut squares in half diagonally once for a total of four corner setting triangles

From cream print, cut:
- 3—2½" strips the width of fabric for binding

Tara's Tips

Many of this book's projects require ¾"-finished half-square triangle units. You can quickly and easily make them with the help of specially printed paper products or computer CDs available at quilt shops. Keep in mind that you may have to adjust the fabric sizes or quantities needed.

SEWING INSTRUCTIONS

Center Block

1. Referring to the following diagram, sew four different light print triangles cut from the 2½" light print squares to opposite sides of a 2¾" medium/dark print square to create a square-in-a-square unit. Press the seams toward the darker fabric.

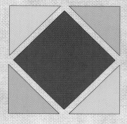 

2. Referring to the following diagram, sew four medium/dark print triangles cut from the 3⅛" squares to the unit from step 1. Press the seams toward the darker fabric.

3. On the wrong side of 14—1⅛" light print squares, mark a diagonal line from corner to corner with a permanent pen, pencil, or chalk marker.

4. With right sides together, layer a marked 1⅛" light print square on top of a 1⅛" medium/dark print square. Sew a scant ¼" seam allowance from both sides of the drawn line.

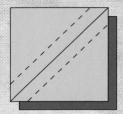

5. Cut the square apart on the drawn line and press the seams open to create a total of two 1¼" square half-square triangle units.

6. Repeat steps 4 and 5 to create a total of 28 half-square triangle units.

7. Sew together six of the half-square triangle units from step 6. To reduce bulk, press the seams open. Repeat to create a second row.

8. Referring to the following diagram, sew together eight half-square triangle units from step 4. Repeat to create a second row.

9. Sew the two rows from step 7 and the two rows from step 8 to the unit from step 2.

Flying Geese Blocks

1. Sew a medium/dark print triangle cut from a 3⅛" medium/dark print square to each of the shorter sides of a larger light print triangle cut from a 4" light print square.

2. Following the instructions for making half-square triangle units on page 60, use 6—1⅝" light print squares and 6—1⅝" medium/dark print squares to make a total of 12 half-square triangle units.

3. Sew three half-square triangle units into a row. Repeat to create a second row.

4. Sew six half-square triangle units into a row, then sew a 1¼" light print square to both ends of that row.

5. Referring to the following diagram, sew the two rows from step 3 to the sides of the Flying Geese unit from step 1.

6. Referring to the following diagram, sew the row from step 4 to the top of the unit from step 5.

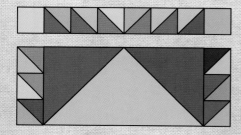

7. Repeat steps 1–6 to create a total of eight Flying Geese blocks.

Square Blocks

1. Sew together one light print triangle cut from a 3⅛" light print square and one medium/dark print triangle cut from a 3⅛" medium/dark print square to create a half-square triangle unit.

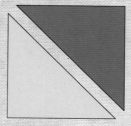

2. Following the instructions for making half-square triangle units on page 60, use 3—1⅝" light print squares and 3—1⅝" medium/dark print squares to create a total of 6 half-square triangle units.

3. Sew together three half-square triangle units.

4. Sew together three half-square triangle units and a 1¼" light print square.

5. Sew the two rows from steps 3 and 4 to the unit from step 1.

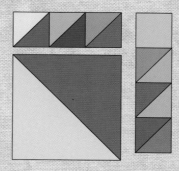

6. Repeat steps 1–5 to create a total of four units like the one in step 5.

Quilt Assembly

1. Referring to the following diagram, lay out the Center block, four Square blocks, eight Flying Geese blocks, four light print setting squares, four light print setting rectangles, and four corner triangles. **NOTE:** the setting squares and rectangles are oversized to create a floating effect for the blocks, which do not touch the edge of the quilt.

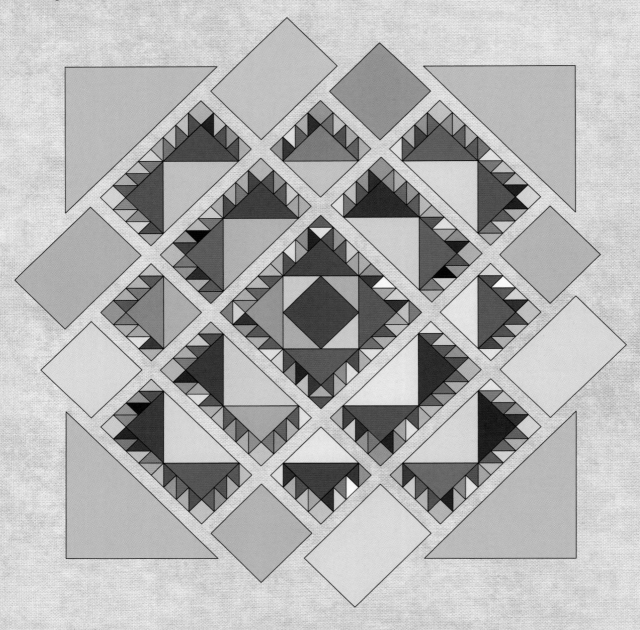

2. Sew the segments from step 1 into rows, then join the five rows and four corner triangles to complete the quilt top.

QUILT ASSEMBLY DIAGRAM

3. Square the quilt top to measure 19½" square so it looks like the finished quilt in the photo on page 57. If you wish, you can leave the top larger, but Tara chose to trim it so there would not be as much excess cream print fabric around the blocks.

4. Sandwich the quilt top, batting, and backing; baste. Quilt as desired, then bind.

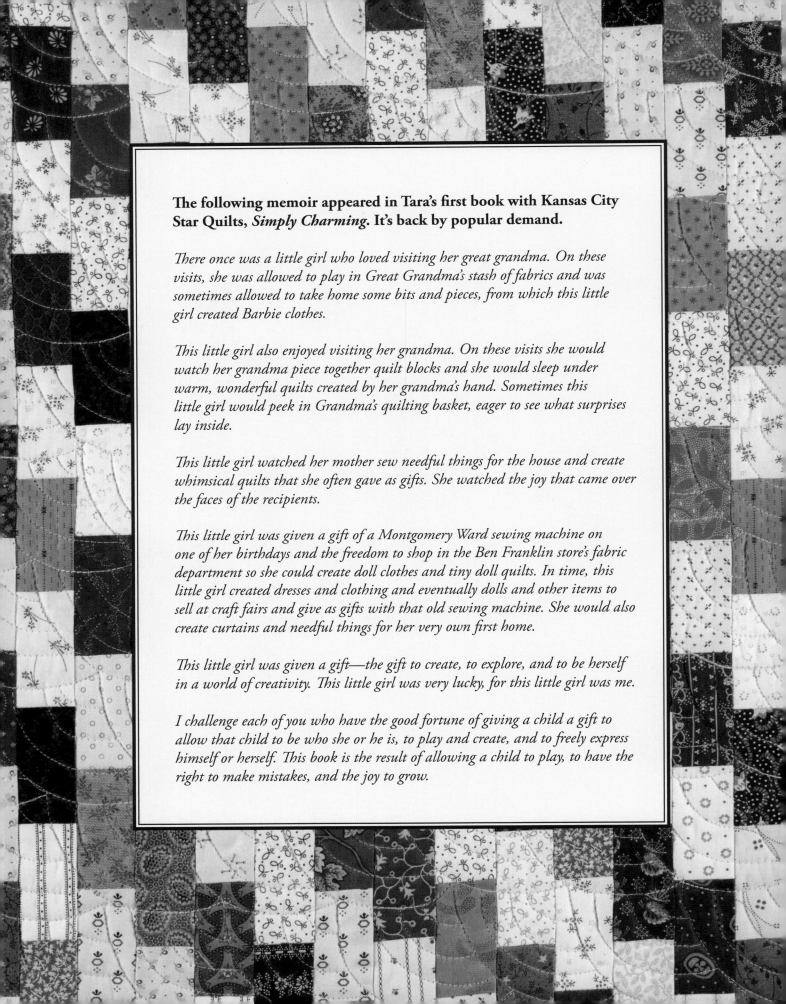

The following memoir appeared in Tara's first book with Kansas City Star Quilts, *Simply Charming*. It's back by popular demand.

There once was a little girl who loved visiting her great grandma. On these visits, she was allowed to play in Great Grandma's stash of fabrics and was sometimes allowed to take home some bits and pieces, from which this little girl created Barbie clothes.

This little girl also enjoyed visiting her grandma. On these visits she would watch her grandma piece together quilt blocks and she would sleep under warm, wonderful quilts created by her grandma's hand. Sometimes this little girl would peek in Grandma's quilting basket, eager to see what surprises lay inside.

This little girl watched her mother sew needful things for the house and create whimsical quilts that she often gave as gifts. She watched the joy that came over the faces of the recipients.

This little girl was given a gift of a Montgomery Ward sewing machine on one of her birthdays and the freedom to shop in the Ben Franklin store's fabric department so she could create doll clothes and tiny doll quilts. In time, this little girl created dresses and clothing and eventually dolls and other items to sell at craft fairs and give as gifts with that old sewing machine. She would also create curtains and needful things for her very own first home.

This little girl was given a gift—the gift to create, to explore, and to be herself in a world of creativity. This little girl was very lucky, for this little girl was me.

I challenge each of you who have the good fortune of giving a child a gift to allow that child to be who she or he is, to play and create, and to freely express himself or herself. This book is the result of allowing a child to play, to have the right to make mistakes, and the joy to grow.

NATIONAL GEOGRAPHIC
L E A R N I N G

National Geographic Learning,
a Cengage Company

Our World 5 Workbook, Second Edition
Series Editors: Joan Kang Shin, JoAnn (Jodi) Crandall

Publisher: Sherrise Roehr
Executive Editor: Eugenia Corbo
Managing Editor: Kellie Cardone
Assistant Editor: Danny Stone
Director of Global Marketing: Ian Martin
Product Marketing Manager: Dave Spain
Heads of Regional Marketing:
  Charlotte Ellis (Europe, Middle East and Africa)
  Kiel Hamm (Asia)
  Irina Pereyra (Latin America)
Content Project Manager: Beth McNally
Media Researcher: Leila Hishmeh
Art Director: Brenda Carmichael
Senior Designer: Lisa Trager
Operations Support: Rebecca G. Barbush,
  Hayley Chwazik-Gee
Manufacturing Planner: Mary Beth Hennebury
Interior Design and Composition:
  DoubleInk Publishing Services

For permission to use material from this text or product,
submit all requests online at **cengage.com/permissions**
Further permissions questions can be emailed to
permissionrequest@cengage.com

ISBN: 978-0-357-03240-4

National Geographic Learning
20 Channel Center Street
Boston, MA 02210
USA

Locate your local office at **international.cengage.com/region**

Visit National Geographic Learning online at **ELTNGL.com**
Visit our corporate website at **www.cengage.com**

Our World Student Resources
(including audio):
ELTNGL.com/ourworld5

ON THE COVER

Puzhehei Lake

Fast Facts
Description: Boats docked in Puzhehei Lake
Length: 2.5 km (1.6 mi.)
Width: 300 m (984 ft.)
Depth: 3 m (9.8 ft)
Name: Puzhehei Lake gets its name from the Yi language and means "pool of fish and shrimp."
©Lin Chen

Printed in the United States of America
Print Number: 10   Print Year: 2024